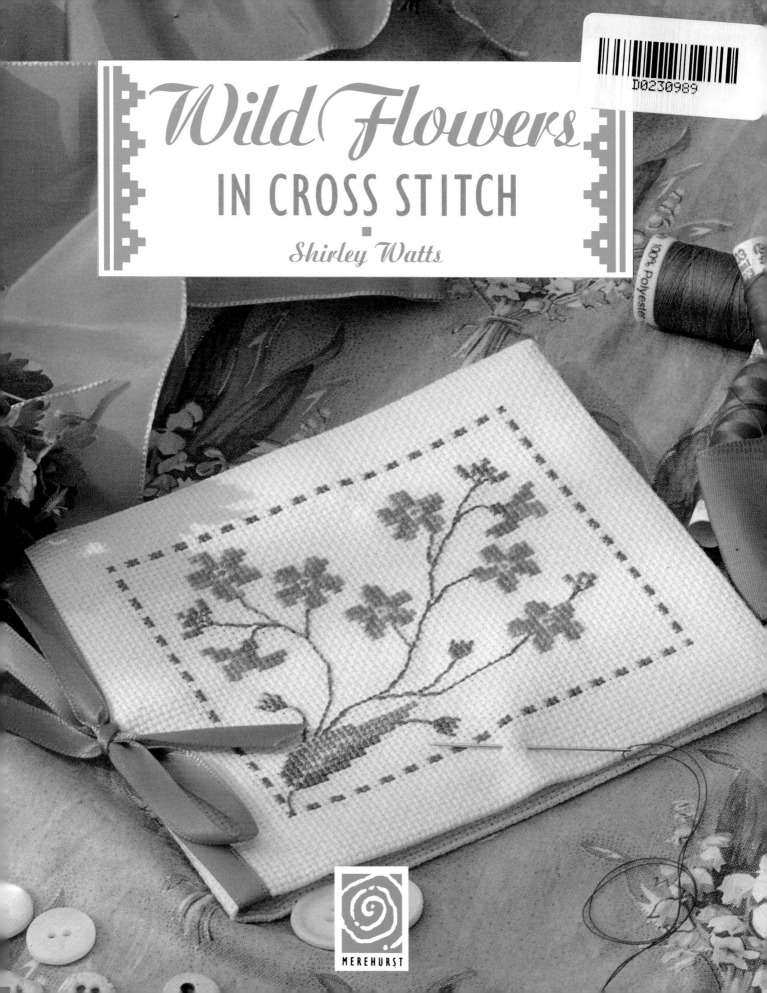

Wild Flowers
IN CROSS STITCH
Shirley Watts

MEREHURST

For Dad, who taught me to observe, draw and photograph nature; and for Mum, who taught me to use a needle with confidence and to appreciate fine stitching.

The projects in this book were all stitched with DMC stranded cotton embroidery threads. The keys given with each chart also list thread combinations for those who wish to use Anchor or Madeira threads. It should be pointed out that the shades produced by different companies vary slightly, and it is not always possible to find identical colours in a different range.

Published in 1993 by Merehurst Limited
Ferry House, 51-57 Lacy Road, Putney, London SW15 1PR
© Copyright 1993 Merehurst Limited
ISBN 1 85391 201 8
Reprinted 1993 (twice)

A catalogue record for this book is available from the British Library.

Managing Editor Heather Dewhurst
Edited by Diana Brinton
Designed by Maggie Aldred
Photography by Debbie Patterson
Illustrations by John Hutchinson
Typesetting by BMD Graphics, Hemel Hempstead
Colour separation by Fotographics Limited, UK – Hong Kong
Printed in Hong Kong by Wing King Tong

Merehurst is the leading publisher of craft books and has an excellent range of titles to suit all levels. Please send to the address above for our free catalogue, stating the title of this book.

CONTENTS

INTRODUCTION

When I was a child, wild flowers grew in profusion in the country lanes, in fields, in woodlands and in the hedgerows. With the advent of herbicides and intensive farming methods, many of these have disappeared in the interest of heavier crop yields, and we are the losers.

Fortunately, there still remain areas of deciduous woodland. Nothing could be more refreshing than the sight and scent of a woodland glade carpeted with bluebells and dotted with red campions.

By designing directly from live specimens, or failing that, from my own photographs, I have tried to capture the essence of those wild flowers and make them as realistic as possible, so each is a recognizable species, and not just another cross-stitch flower.

The projects vary in difficulty from the very simple to much more elaborate ones. For the beginner, there are floral cards and gift tags, and various fragrant sachets. As you gain in confidence, you may like to try the larger projects such as the cushion and matching wall hanger, or the panel of six wayside flowers.

The patterns have been worked on various materials, ranging from perforated paper to fabrics, with between 22 and 14 threads per 2.5cm (1in). More experienced cross stitchers may like to experiment by working the designs on different counts from those suggested – to suit their eyesight – but in this case it is important that you calculate the size of your completed design before you begin.

I hope you have a lot of pleasure stitching these designs, and as you complete each one I hope it will bring a breath of the countryside into your home.   Happy stitching!

BASIC SKILLS

BEFORE YOU BEGIN

PREPARING THE FABRIC
Even with an average amount of handling, many evenweave fabrics tend to fray at the edges, so it is a good idea to overcast the raw edges, using ordinary sewing thread, before you begin.

THE INSTRUCTIONS
Each project begins with a full list of the materials that you will require; Aida, Tula, Lugana and Linda are all fabrics produced by Zweigart. Note that the measurements given for the embroidery fabric include a minimum of 3cm (1¼in) all around to allow for stretching it in a frame and preparing the edges to prevent them from fraying.

Colour keys for stranded embroidery cottons – DMC, Anchor or Madeira – are given with each chart. It is assumed that you will need to buy one skein of each colour mentioned in a particular key, even though you may use less, but where two or more skeins are needed, this information is included in the main list of requirements.

To work from the charts, particularly those where several symbols are used in close proximity, some readers may find it helpful to have the chart enlarged so that the squares and symbols can be seen more easily. Many photocopying services will do this for a minimum charge.

Before you begin to embroider, always mark the centre of the design with two lines of basting stitches, one vertical and one horizontal, running from edge to edge of the fabric, as indicated by the arrows on the charts.

As you stitch, use the centre lines given on the chart and the basting threads on your fabric as reference points for counting the squares and threads to position your design accurately.

WORKING IN A HOOP
A hoop is the most popular frame for use with small areas of embroidery. It consists of two rings, one fitted inside the other; the outer ring usually has an

tightened to hold the stretched fabric in place. Hoops are available in several sizes, ranging from 10cm (4in) in diameter to quilting hoops with a diameter of 38cm (15in). Hoops with table stands or floor stands attached are also available.

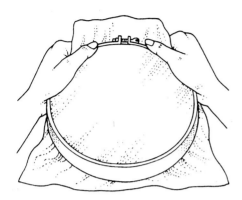

1 To stretch your fabric in a hoop, place the area to be embroidered over the inner ring and press the outer ring over it with the tension screw released. Tissue paper can be placed between the outer ring and the embroidery, so that the hoop does not mark the fabric. Lay the tissue paper over the fabric when you set it in the hoop, then tear away the central, embroidery area.

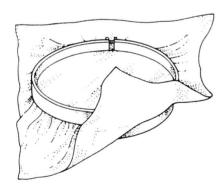

2 Smooth the fabric and, if needed, straighten the grain before tightening the screw. The fabric should be evenly stretched.

EXTENDING EMBROIDERY FABRIC
It is easy to extend a piece of embroidery fabric, such as a bookmark, to stretch it in a hoop.

● Fabric oddments of a similar weight can be used. Simply cut four pieces to size (in other words, to the measurement that will fit both the embroidery fabric and your hoop) and baste them to each side

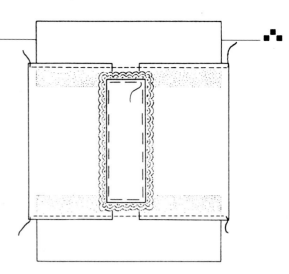

of the embroidery fabric before stretching it in the hoop in the usual way.

WORKING IN A RECTANGULAR FRAME
Rectangular frames are more suitable for larger pieces of embroidery. They consist of two rollers, with tapes attached, and two flat side pieces, which slot into the rollers and are held in place by pegs or screw attachments. Available in different sizes, either alone or with adjustable table or floor stands, frames are measured by the length of the roller tape, and range in size from 30cm (12in) to 68cm (27in).

As alternatives to a slate frame, canvas stretchers and the backs of old picture frames can be used. Provided there is sufficient extra fabric around the finished size of the embroidery, the edges can be turned under and simply attached with drawing pins (thumb tacks) or staples.

1 To stretch your fabric in a rectangular frame, cut out the fabric, allowing at least an extra 5cm (2in) all around the finished size of the embroidery. Baste a single 12mm (½in) turning on the top and bottom edges and oversew strong tape, 2.5cm (1in) wide, to the other two sides. Mark the centre line both ways with basting stitches. Working from the centre outwards and using strong thread, oversew the top and bottom edges to the roller tapes. Fit the side pieces into the slots, and roll any extra fabric on one roller until the fabric is taut.

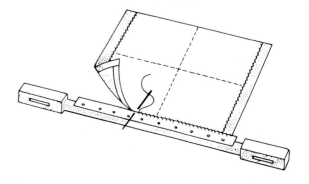

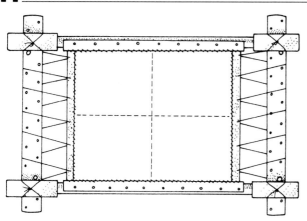

2 Insert the pegs or adjust the screw attachments to secure the frame. Thread a large-eyed needle (chenille needle) with strong thread or fine string and lace both edges, securing the ends around the intersections of the frame. Lace the webbing at 2.5cm (1in) intervals, stretching the fabric evenly.

ENLARGING A GRAPH PATTERN

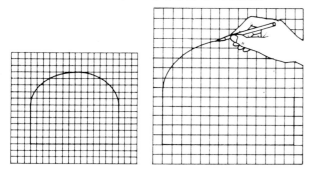

● To enlarge a graph pattern, you will need a sheet of graph paper ruled in 1cm (⅜in) squares, a ruler and pencil. If, for example, the scale is one square to 5cm (2in) you should first mark the appropriate lines to give a grid of the correct size. Copy the graph freehand from the small grid to the larger one, completing one square at a time. Use a ruler to draw the straight lines first, and then copy the freehand curves.

TO BIND AN EDGE

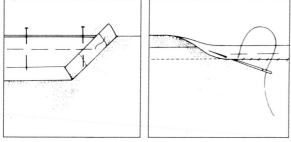

1 Open out the turning on one edge of the bias binding and pin in position on the right side of the fabric, matching the fold to the seamline. Fold over the cut end of the binding. Finish by overlapping the starting point by about 12mm (½in). Baste and machine stitch along the seamline.

2 Fold the binding over the raw edge to the wrong side, baste and, using matching sewing thread, neatly hem to finish.

PIPED SEAMS

Contrasting piping adds a special decorative finish to a seam and looks particularly attractive on items such as cushions and cosies.

You can cover piping cord with either bias-cut fabric of your choice or a bias binding; alternatively, ready-covered piping cord is available in several widths and many colours.

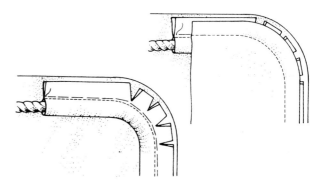

1 To apply piping, pin and baste it to the right side of the fabric, with seam lines matching. Clip into the seam allowance where necessary.

2 With right sides together, place the second piece of fabric on top, enclosing the piping. Baste and then either hand stitch in place or machine stitch, using a zipper foot. Stitch as close to the piping as possible, covering the first line of stitching.

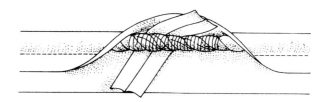

3 To join ends of piping cord together, first overlap the two ends by about 2.5cm (1in). Unpick the two cut ends of bias to reveal the cord. Join the bias strip as shown. Trim and press the seam open. Unravel and splice the two ends of the cord. Fold the bias strip over it, and finish basting around the edge.

MOUNTING EMBROIDERY

The cardboard should be cut to the size of the finished embroidery, with an extra 6mm (¼in) added all around to allow for the recess in the frame.

LIGHTWEIGHT FABRICS

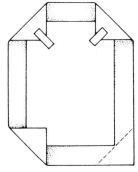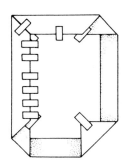

1 Place the emboidery face down, with the cardboard centred on top, and basting and pencil lines matching. Begin by folding over the fabric at each corner and securing it with masking tape.

2 Working first on one side and then the other, fold over the fabric on all sides and secure it firmly with pieces of masking tape, placed about 2.5cm (1in) apart. Also neaten the mitred corners with masking tape, pulling the fabric tightly to give a firm, smooth finish.

HEAVIER FABRICS

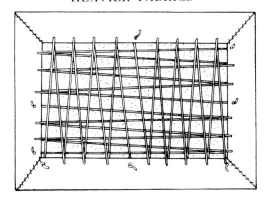

● Lay the embroidery face down, with the cardboard centred on top; fold over the edges of the fabric on opposite sides, making mitred folds at the corners, and lace across, using strong thread. Repeat on the other two sides. Finally, pull up the stitches fairly tightly to stretch the fabric firmly over the cardboard. Overstitch the mitred corners.

CROSS STITCH

For all cross stitch embroidery, the following two methods of working are used. In each case, neat rows of vertical stitches are produced on the back of the fabric.

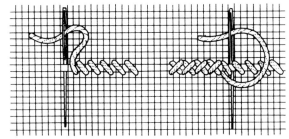

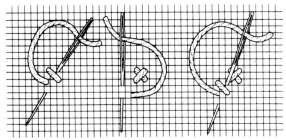

● When stitching large areas, work in horizontal rows. Working from right to left, complete the first row of evenly spaced diagonal stitches over the number of threads specified in the project instructions. Then, working from left to right, repeat the process. Continue in this way, making sure each stitch crosses in the same direction.

● When stitching diagonal lines, work downwards, completing each stitch before moving to the next.

BACKSTITCH

Backstitch is used in the projects to give emphasis to a particular foldline, an outline or a shadow. The stitches are worked over the same number of threads as the cross stitch, forming continuous straight or diagonal lines.

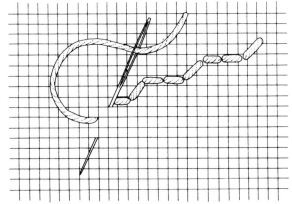

● Make the first stitch from left to right; pass the needle behind the fabric, and bring it out one stitch length ahead to the left. Repeat and continue in this way along the line.

Foxglove Duo

This beautiful cushion would enhance
any sitting room, and to add that extra
dimension, why not complement it
with an elegant wall hanger?

FOXGLOVE DUO

YOU WILL NEED

For the Foxglove cushion cover, measuring 47cm (18½in) square:

52cm (21in) of cream Aida fabric, with 14 threads to 2.5cm (1in)
48.5cm (19½in) square of furnishing fabric, for the cushion back
Two 48.5cm (19½in) squares of strong unbleached cotton fabric, for the inner cover
Stranded embroidery cotton in the colours given in the panel
No24 tapestry needle
3m (3½yds) of matching green (or deep pink) cushion cord, 6mm (¼in) in diameter
47cm (18½in) cushion pad

For the Wall hanging, measuring 41cm × 16.5cm (16½in × 6½in):

50cm × 25cm (20in × 10in) of cream Aida fabric, with 18 threads to 2.5cm (1in)
46cm × 20.5cm (18in × 8in) of cream lining fabric
40.5cm × 16cm (16in × 6¼in) of iron-on interfacing
Stranded embroidery cotton in the colours given in the panel
No26 tapestry needle
Pair of wooden hangers (for suppliers, see page 48)

●

THE EMBROIDERY

Prepare the fabric for your chosen design, marking the centre lines with basting stitches, and mount it in a frame (see page 5). In both cases, start to embroider from the centre of the design. For the cushion, use three strands of cotton in the needle for both the cross stitch and the backstitch.

The wall hanging is adapted from the cushion design, as seen in the picture. The stalk of the Timothy grass on the left-hand side is lowered so that it extends only over 32 threads from the upper leaf to the head: this is to balance the effect. Use two strands of thread in the needle for cross stitching and backstitching the grass stalks, and one thread for backstitching the finer details.

When you have finished your chosen design, gently steam press on the wrong side.

MAKING THE CUSHION COVER

With right sides together, and taking a 12mm (½in) seam, join the two pieces of strong cotton for the inner lining, leaving a 25cm (10in) opening at one side. Trim across the corners and turn the lining inside out. Insert the cushion pad and slipstitch the opening.

Trim the embroidered fabric to measure 48.5cm (19½in) square, keeping the design centred. Remove the central basting lines and, with right sides together, join the embroidered fabric and the cover backing fabric, again leaving a 25cm (10in) opening. Repeat the same process as for the inner lining.

To complete the cover, trim the edges with cord, forming it into loops at the corners and slipstitching it in place.

THE WALL HANGING

Centre the interfacing on the back of the embroidery and pin it in place. Remove the basting stitches and iron the interfacing in position. Trim the long edges of the embroidery until it measures 19cm (7½in) wide. Turn in the long edges by 12mm (½in) and press.

On the two short edges, make a 6mm (¼in) turning. Make a second turning, 4cm (1½in) deep, taking the fabric over a rod at the top and bottom. Baste and neatly hem in place.

Turn in the long edges of the lining fabric by 12mm (½in) and turn in the short edges so that the piece will neatly cover all raw edges and hems at the back of the work. Slipstitch in place.

FOXGLOVE CUSHION ▶		DMC	ANCHOR	MADEIRA
·	Cream	746	275	0101
I	Rose pink	3609	85	0710
⋮	Medium rose	3608	86	0709
т	Deep rose	3607	87	0708
x	Dull pink	223	894	0812
⊥	Dusky pink	778	968	0808
U	Purplish red	315	896	0810
⊣	Lime green	472	264	1414
⊣	Bluish green	320	216	1311
	Pale green*	522	859	1513
−	Green	3348	264	1409
Y	Medium green	3347	266	1408
+	Dark green	3346	262	1407
⊐	Very dark green	3345	268	1406
⌐	Light fawn	3047	886	2205
⊢	Fawn	612	832	2108

Note: bks foxglove bells in purplish red, Timothy grass stalks and leaf in bluish green and seeds in lime green, bent grass stalk in pale green*, ground elder flower stalks in dark green, red campion stalks and flower in green, and style of dead foxglove flower in deep rose; for the wallhanger, you will not need dull pink, dusky pink, fawn, light fawn, pale green, very dark green, and green.

Gift Tags and Bookmark

These little hand-made tags will enhance any gift by adding that special personal touch. In this group of designs, the wild pansy and the red campion are accompanied by the meadow cranesbill, a member of the geranium family.

GIFT TAGS AND BOOKMARK

YOU WILL NEED

For the Meadow Cranesbill bookmark, measuring
20.5cm × 7.5cm (8in × 3in):

*25cm × 11.5cm (10in × 4½in) of white
perforated paper, with 14 divisions to 2.5cm (1in)
20.5cm × 7.5cm (8in × 3in) of iron-on
interfacing
50cm (20in) of lilac ribbon, 6mm (¼in) wide
Stranded embroidery cotton in the colours given
in the appropriate panel
No24 tapestry needle*

For the Red Campion gift tag, measuring
9.5cm × 5cm (3¾in × 2in):

*19cm × 5cm (7½in × 2in) of white perforated
paper, with 14 divisions to 2.5cm (1in)
19cm × 5cm (7½in × 2in) of parchment paper,
for the inside
Stranded embroidery cotton in the colours given
in the appropriate panel
No24 tapestry needle*

For either the Meadow Cranesbill or the Wild
Pansy gift tag, each measuring 5cm (2in):

*10cm (4in) of cream Aida fabric, with 22 threads
to 2.5cm (1in)
Stranded embroidery cotton in the colours given
in the appropriate panel
No26 tapestry needle
Gift tag (for suppliers, see page 48)*

THE EMBROIDERY

For the designs embroidered on perforated paper, use three strands of thread in the needle. Find the centre of the bookmark paper by counting the spaces between the holes. Fold the paper for the tag in half, and find the centre of the front half only. In either case, mark the centre with a soft pencil, which can be rubbed out later. Begin from the centre point of the pattern and work outward.

The design for the meadow cranesbill tag is simply the top flower from the bookmark design. For this and the wild pansy tag, use one strand of thread in the needle for both cross stitch and back-stitch, and embroider from the centre. Gently steam press the embroidery on the wrong side.

FINISHING THE BOOKMARK

Centre the interfacing on the wrong side of the book-mark, then iron it in place. Trim around the border of the design, leaving an edging of two perforations. You may find it easier to mark your cutting line with a soft pencil before you start.

Cut the ribbon in half. Gather along the edge of one piece and tighten it into a rosette. Fold the other length in half to make two streamers and stitch the fold to the lower edge of the bookmark. Glue or stitch the rosette in place over the streamers.

MAKING THE GIFT TAGS

For the red campion gift tags, use all-purpose adhesive to glue the parchment paper to the back of the embroidered paper. Fold the tag in half.

For the meadow cranesbill or wild pansy tag, trim around the design until the fabric measures 4.5cm (1¾in) square. Open the tag and centre the design in the aperture, then secure according to the manufac-turer's instructions.

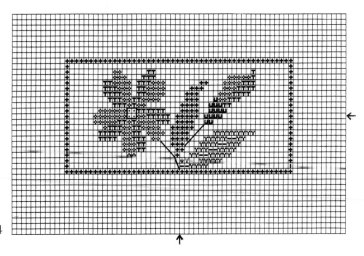

RED CAMPION ◄		DMC	ANCHOR	MADEIRA
I	Pale pink	3609	85	0710
∴	Pink	3608	86	0709
T	Deep pink	3607	87	0708
Ц	Purplish red	315	896	0810
—	Pale green	3348	264	1409
Y	Green	3347	266	1408
+	Dark green	3346	262	1407

Note: bks stalks and flower centre in green.

MEADOW CRANESBILL ▶		DMC	ANCHOR	MADEIRA
·	Pale mauve	211	342	0801
⊥	Mauve	210	108	0802
I	Pale lavender blue	341	117	0901
x	Blue	340	118	0902
∻	Medium blue	794	120	0907
ჟ	Lime green	471	266	1501
⅃	Green	3363	262	1602
+	Dark green	501	878	1704
−	Fawn	613	831	2109
T	Greenish brown	611	898	2107
U	Dark brown	898	360	2006
■	Black	310	403	Black

Note: bks outline the centre of the upper flower in black, the petals of the lower flower in blue, seed pods in dark brown and stems and centre of upper flower in green; for the gift tag, buy only those colours indicated on the chart.

WILD PANSY ▼		DMC	ANCHOR	MADEIRA
▫	White*	White	2	White
−	Light mauve	554	97	0711
⅃	Medium mauve	552	101	0713
x	Dark mauve	550	102	0714
·	Yellow	726	295	0109
+	Dark green	3346	262	1407
■	Black	310	403	Black

Note: outline flower centres in white.*

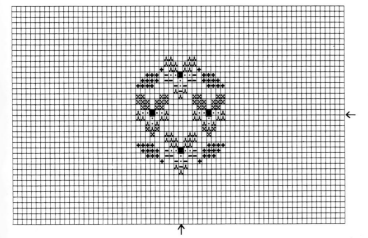

Framed
Fruits

The briar rose, also known as
eglantine, is a fragrant wild hedgerow
rose, much pinker than the common
dog rose. In the autumn it bears shiny
red hips, rich in vitamin C.
The bramble is also a member of the
rose family, with white or pale pink
flowers in early summer, giving way to
a profusion of ripened berries
later in the year.

FRAMED FRUITS

YOU WILL NEED

For each picture, set in a frame with a picture area measuring 18cm × 12.5cm (7in × 5in):

27cm × 23cm (10¾in × 9in) of eau-de-Nil Aida fabric, with 18 threads to 2.5cm (1in)
Stranded embroidery cotton in the colours given in the panel
No26 tapestry needle
Strong thread, for lacing across the back
Cross-over frame (for suppliers, see page 48)

●

THE EMBROIDERY

For each picture, prepare the fabric, marking the centre lines of the design with basting stitches, and set it in a frame (see page 5). Start your embroidery from the centre of the design, completing the main areas first, and then the backstitching. Use two strands of thread for both the cross stitch and back-stitching, except for fine details, such as the stamens, where one thread is recommended.

Gently steam press the finished embroidery on the wrong side. It is helpful to retain the central basting stitches at this stage.

ASSEMBLING THE PICTURES

Each picture is assembled in the same way. Trim the edges of the embroidery until it measures 23cm × 18cm (9in × 7¼in). Mark the central horizontal and vertical lines on the mount provided and, matching these with the central basting stitches, lace the embroidery over the mount, following the instructions on page 6. Carefully remove the basting stitches.

Complete the assembly according to the manufacturer's instructions.

BRIAR ROSE ◄

		DMC	ANCHOR	MADEIRA
⌐	White	White	2	White
·	Cream	712	926	2101
⌐	Palest pink	3689	49	0607
I	Pale pink	605	60	0613
∴	Pink	604	66	0614
+	Deep pink	603	62	0701
⊣	Lemon	744	301	0112
ↄ	Yellow	743	297	0113
◢	Bright yellow	972	298	0107
x	Orange	970	316	0204
‖	Deep orange	900	333	0208
⊢	Green	3347	266	1408
⊥	Medium green	3346	262	1407
⊤	Dark green	3345	268	1406
—	Yellowish green	472	264	1414
	Dark yellowish green*	470	267	1503
⌐	Fawn	729	890	2209
⊐	Yellowish brown	831	889	2201

Note: bks rosehips in dark yellowish green*, stamens in yellow, pollen tips on stamens, adjacent flower centre and dying leaf in yellowish brown, leaf stalks in dark green, and rosehip stalks in medium green.

BRAMBLE ▼

		DMC	ANCHOR	MADEIRA
·	White	White	2	White
╱	Soft pink	819	271	0501
⌐	Pink	3688	66	0605
⊤	Deep pink	3350	42	0603
—	Pale mauve	3609	85	0710
x	Purplish pink	3608	86	0709
⊐	Navy	939	152	1009
⊢	Pale green	3013	842	1605
I	Green	3363	262	1602
+	Dark green	520	862	1514
⅃	Yellowish green	3348	264	1409
∴	Greyish green	3052	859	1509
⊣	Ginger brown	433	371	2008
⊔	Dark brown	3031	905	2003
⊥	Dark grey	413	401	1713
■	Black	310	403	Black

Note: bks base of new fruit in ginger brown, tips of stamens and base of flowers in dark green, stamens in pale green and all stems in yellowish green.

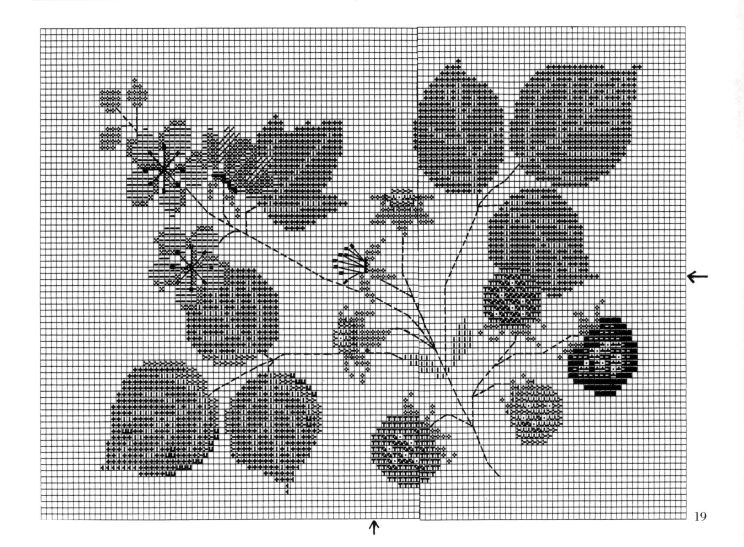

Floral Greetings Cards

Anyone would be delighted to receive
one of these charming flower
portraits, with two matching tags
as shown on page 12.

FLORAL GREETINGS CARDS

YOU WILL NEED

For the Red Campion card, measuring
20.5cm × 15cm (8in × 6in), with a rectangular
portrait cut-out measuring 14cm × 9cm
(5½in × 3½in):

*18cm × 14cm (7¼in × 5½in) of cream Aida
fabric, with 18 threads to 2.5cm (1in)
18cm × 14cm (7¼in × 5½in) of iron-on
interfacing
Stranded embroidery cotton in the colours given
in the appropriate panel
No26 tapestry needle
Greetings card blank (for suppliers, see page 48)*

For the Bluebell card, measuring 20.5cm × 15cm
(8in × 6in), with an oval cut-out measuring
14cm × 9cm (5½in × 3½in):

*18cm × 14cm (7¼in × 5½in) of cream Aida
fabric, with 18 threads to 2.5cm (1in)
18cm × 14cm (7¼in × 5½in) of iron-on
interfacing
Stranded embroidery cotton in the colours given
in the appropriate panel
No26 tapestry needle
Greetings card blank (for suppliers, see page 48)*

For the Wild Pansy card, measuring 12cm × 9cm
(4¾in × 3½in), with an oval cut-out measuring
8.5cm × 6.5cm (3¼in × 2½in):

*13.5cm × 9cm (5¼in × 3½in) of cream Aida
fabric, with 18 threads to 2.5cm (1in)
13.5cm × 9cm (5¼in × 3½in) of iron-on
interfacing
Stranded embroidery cotton in the colours given
in the appropriate panel
No26 tapestry needle
Greetings card blank (for suppliers, see page 48)*

•
•

THE EMBROIDERY

All three cards are stitched in the same way and
on the same type of fabric.

Note that it is particularly important with
embroidered cards to avoid excessive overstitching

on the back, as this would cause unsightly lumps
to show through on the right side.

Prepare the fabric, marking the centre lines of
each design with basting stitches, and mount it
in a hoop, following the instructions on page 5.
Referring to the appropriate chart, complete the
cross stitching, using two strands in the needle
throughout. Embroider the main areas first, and
then finish with the backstitching. If necessary,
steam press on the wrong side.

MAKING UP THE CARDS

Iron the interfacing to the back of the embroidery,
and trim both to about 12mm (½in) larger all around
than the cut-out window. This will help to prevent
the mounted picture from wrinkling. Position the
embroidery behind the window.

Open out the self-adhesive mount and centre your
embroidery behind the aperture. Fold the card and
press firmly to secure. Some cards require a dab of
glue to ensure a secure and neat finish.

WILD PANSY ▼		DMC	ANCHOR	MADEIRA
	White*	White	2	White
–	Light mauve	554	97	0711
⌐	Medium mauve	552	101	0713
x	Dark mauve	550	102	0714
·	Yellow	726	295	0109
+	Dark green	3346	817	1407
■	Black	310	403	Black

Note: bks outline of flower centres in white*.

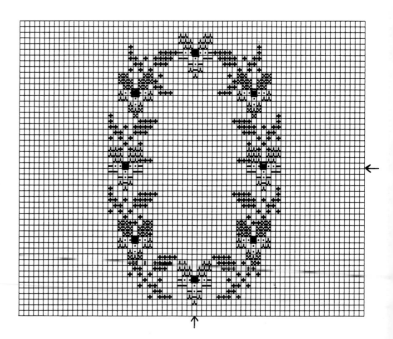

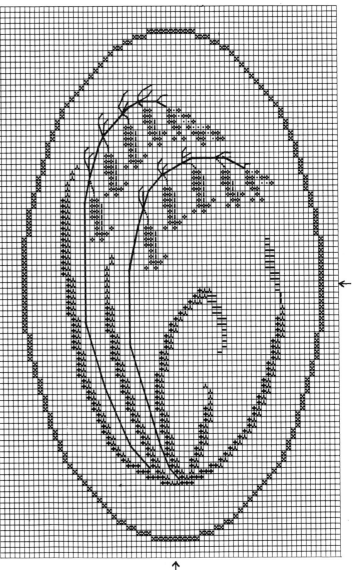

RED CAMPION ▼		DMC	ANCHOR	MADEIRA
I	Pale pink	3609	85	0710
⊹	Pink	3608	86	0709
⊤	Deep pink	3607	87	0708
U	Purplish red	315	896	0810
–	Pale green	3348	264	1409
Ï	Green	3347	266	1408
+	Dark green	3346	817	1407

Note: bks flower stems and centres in green.

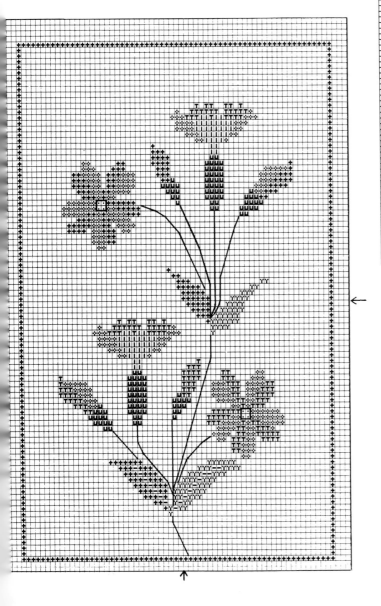

BLUEBELL ▲		DMC	ANCHOR	MADEIRA
·	Light mauve	210	108	0802
I	Pale blue	341	117	0901
⊹	Blue	340	118	0902
X	Light navy	792	177	0905
–	Light green	3347	266	1408
⌐	Medium green	3346	817	1407
+	Dark green	3345	268	1406

Note: bks flowers stalks in light mauve, bracts in pale blue, leaf blade in dark green, and main stems in light green.

Silverweed Table Set

Potentilla anserina (silverweed) is used for an elegant design for a place setting for one. A complete set would make the perfect gift for a golden wedding anniversary. Silverweed is an attractive yellow-flowered roadside plant, with leaves that are a delicate silvery green on the underside. It flowers in the summer months, thriving in dampish conditions.

SILVERWEED TABLE SET

YOU WILL NEED

For one placemat, measuring 46cm × 34cm
(18½in × 13½in):

*50cm × 39cm (20in × 15½in) of cream
evenweave fabric, with 28 threads to 2.5cm (1in)
Stranded embroidery cotton in the colours given
in the panel
No26 tapestry needle*

For one napkin, measuring 37cm (14½) square:

*42cm (16½in) of cream evenweave fabric, with
28 threads to 2.5cm (1in)
Stranded embroidery cotton in the colours given
in the panel
No26 tapestry needle*

*Alternatively, ready-prepared placemats and
napkins can be obtained from specialist
suppliers (see page 48)*

•

THE EMBROIDERY

For either the placemat or the napkin, begin by
preparing the edges of the fabric in the usual way
(see page 4).

For the placemat, mark the central horizontal
line across the fabric with a line of basting stitches.
From the left-hand side of the fabric, measure in
along this line for 10cm (4in). A vertical line at this
point marks the start of the embroidery. Set the
fabric in a frame (see page 5), and work out from
the central point to complete two motifs, one on
either side of the horizontal line.

For the napkin, which features only one motif,
baste a vertical line 10cm (4in) in from the left-
hand side and a horizontal one 13.5cm (5¼in) up
from the lower edge. The centre point of the motif
is the point where these two lines intersect.

For both the placemat and the napkin, use three
strands of embroidery cotton in the needle for the
cross stitch and the backstitching, working over two
fabric threads. Gently steam press the finished
embroideries on the wrong side.

FRINGING

Trim 2.5cm (1in) all around the finished embroideries, so that the placemat measures 46cm × 34cm
(18½in × 13½in) and the napkin measures 37cm
(14½in) square.

On all four sides of each, withdraw a single fabric
thread 12mm (½in) in from the outer edge.

The fringing can be secured in one of several
ways: by machining around the rectangle (placemat)
or square (napkin) left by the withdrawn threads,
using either straight stitch or a narrow zigzag stitch;
by overcasting every alternate thread by hand, or by
hemstitching, as shown below.

When you have secured the line by your chosen
method, remove all cross threads below the stitched
line to complete the fringe.

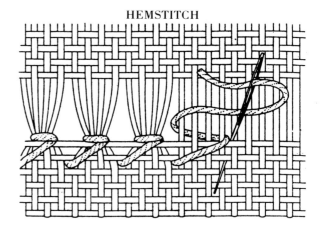

HEMSTITCH

If you prefer to secure your fringing by hemstitch,
remove a single thread from the fabric at the hem-
line (the start of the fringe). Bring the needle out on
the right side, two threads below the drawn-thread
line. Working from left to right, pick up either two or
three threads, as shown in the diagram. Bring the
needle out again and insert it behind the fabric, to
emerge two threads down, ready to make the next
stitch. Before reinserting the needle, pull the thread
tight, so that the bound threads form a neat group. To
complete the fringe, remove the weft threads below
the hemstitching.

SILVERWEED ◄	DMC	ANCHOR	MADEIRA
· Yellow	727	293	0110
▬ Deep yellow	726	295	0109
✘ Gold	725	306	0113
ϒ Silver green	368	240	1310
∴ Light green	3347	266	1408
✚ Green	3346	262	1407
Ա Ginger brown	782	308	2212

Note: bks flower stems, outlines and centres in ginger brown, and leaf stalks in light green.

A Panel of Flowers

This panel of wayside flowers, with their delicate hues, will bring a touch of the countryside to your home. You might choose to mount it in a frame, as shown, or to make it into a cushion as a partner for the foxglove cushion (see page 8). Indeed, the design is so adaptable that you can take any section and turn it into a beautiful greetings card for the discerning lover of wild flowers.

A PANEL OF FLOWERS

YOU WILL NEED

For this panel, here with a frame measurement of
39.5cm × 37cm (15¾in × 14½in):

47cm × 43.5cm (19in × 17½in) of cream Aida,
with 18 threads to 2.5cm (1in)
Stranded embroidery cotton in the colours given
in the panel
No26 tapestry needle

Strong cardboard, for the mount, sufficient to fit
into the frame recess
Strong thread, for lacing across the back when
mounting
Picture frame of your choice

NOTE To complete the sampler, you will only
need one skein each of every colour listed in the
combined six charts, with the exception of green
(3346/817/1407), for which you will
require two skeins.

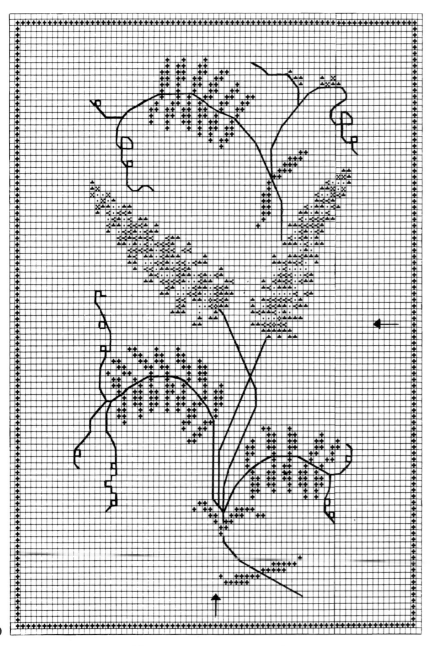

Chart 1 Tufted Vetch

TUFTED VETCH ◀		DMC	ANCHOR	MADEIRA
x	Pink	3608	86	0709
·	Pale mauve	211	342	0801
⊷	Medium mauve	554	97	0711
⊥	Deep mauve	553	98	0712
⁖	Light green	3347	266	1408
+	Green	3346	262	1407
Note: use light green for bks.				

THE EMBROIDERY

Prepare the edges of the fabric in the usual way. The six panels of the design are shown on separate charts, so the centre lines of each must be marked. Start by marking the horizontal and vertical centre lines of the fabric with basting stitches. The border around each flower study measures 99 stitches (in total) down each side and 75 stitches (in total) along the top and bottom, and there are two threads between each border. You may find it easier to work out where to place the centre basting lines if you lightly mark the border outlines on the back of the fabric with a soft pencil.

With the fabric held in a frame (see page 5), work from the centre point of each chart to complete the panels one by one. Start with the two central panels, top and bottom, and check that you have the positioning correct before going on to complete the four corner panels. Use two strands of embroidery cotton in the needle for both the cross stitch and the backstitching, with the exceptions of fine details, such as stamens, which are stitched with one thread, as on the charts.

When you have completed the embroidery, gently steam press it on the wrong side. Leave the two central lines of basting stitches in place, but remove those at either side.

Chart 2 Red Clover

RED CLOVER ▶	DMC	ANCHOR	MADEIRA
⌊ Pale pink	3609	85	0710
X Pink	3608	86	0709
⊣ Deep pink	3607	87	0708
⊐ Purplish red	315	896	0810
◥ Silver green	524	858	1511
⊢ Yellowish green	472	264	1414
⸫ Pale moss green	734	279	1610
⊔ Medium moss green	733	280	1611
⊦ Medium green	3363	262	1602
◢ Dark green	936	269	1507

Note: use medium green for bks.

MOUNTING THE PANEL

Mark the central horizontal and vertical lines on the cardboard and align these with the lines of basting stitches. Lace the embroidery over the mount, following the instructions on page 6, and remove basting stitches.

Set the mount in a frame of your choice. The one used here was intentionally selected for its unobtrusive simplicity, but a narrow silvered frame might be equally effective.

As an alternative idea, the flower portraits might be embroidered and framed individually to make a matching set, perhaps for a guest room.

The flowers chosen – tufted vetch (*Vicia cracca*), red clover (*Trifolium pratense*), chicory (*Cichorium intybus*), rosebay willowherb (*Epilobium angustifolium*), harebell (*Campanula rotundifolia*) and field scabious (*Knautia arvensis*) – are all ones that you might find by the wayside when walking on a summer's afternoon.

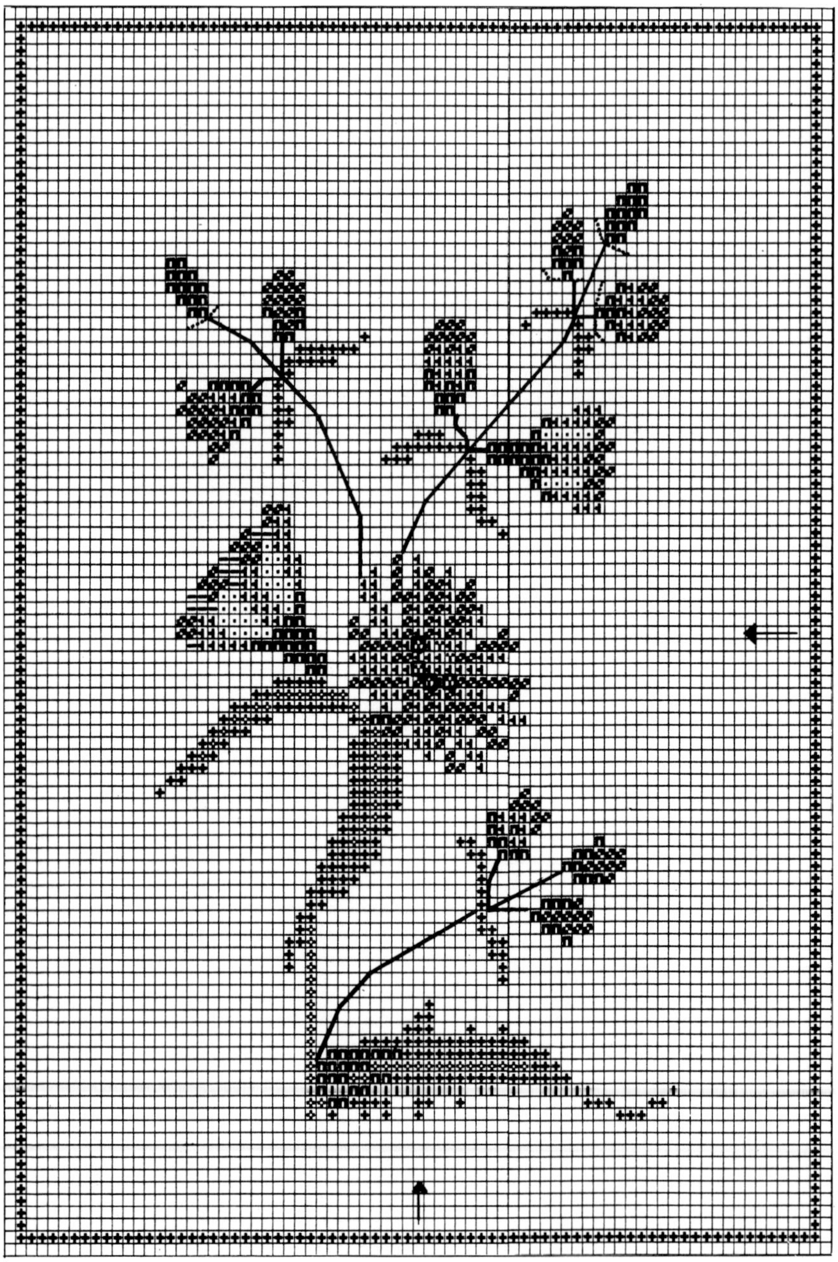

Chart 3 Chicory

CHICORY ◀	DMC	ANCHOR	MADEIRA
┳ Cream	746	275	0101
· Pale mauve	211	342	0801
⊣ Mauve	210	108	0802
Deep mauve*	553	98	0712
– Pale blue	341	117	0901
▪ Blue	340	118	0902
⁘ Light green	3347	266	1408
+ Green	3346	262	1407
⊓ Dark green	520	862	1514

Note: bks bracts in dark green, flower centre in deep mauve, and main stems in light green.*

Chart 4 Rosebay Willowherb

ROSEBAY WILLOWHERB ▶		DMC	ANCHOR	MADEIRA
	Cream*	746	275	0101
⌡	Pale pink	3609	85	0710
✗	Pink	3608	86	0709
⊣	Deep pink	3607	87	0708
⊐	Purplish red	315	896	0810
∴	Light green	3347	266	1408
⌐	Moss green	522	859	1513
⊢	Medium green	3363	262	1602
⊓	Dark green	520	862	1514

Note: bks flower centres and stamens in cream, main stem and style in light green, top of seed pod and stalks in deep pink, and bud and flower stalks in pink.

HAREBELL ▼		DMC	ANCHOR	MADEIRA
I	Pale blue	794	120	0907
⊥	Medium blue	793	121	0906
╱	Dark blue	792	940	0905
⋮	Light green	3347	266	1408
+	Green	3346	262	1407

Note: bks bracts in green and flower and leaf stems in light green.

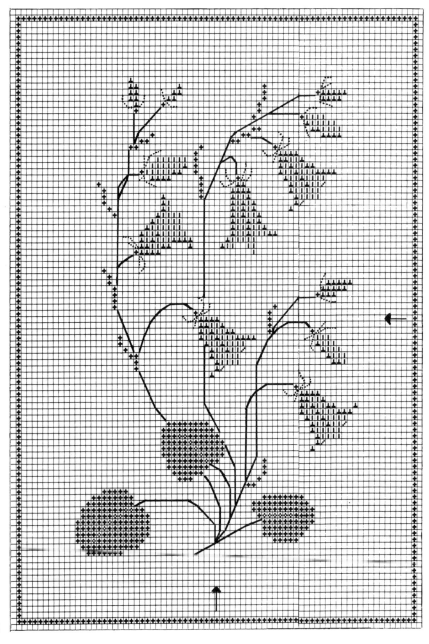

Chart 5 Harebell

1 Tufted Vetch	2 Red Clover	3 Chicory
4 Rosebay Willowherb	5 Harebell	6 Field Scabious

FIELD SCABIOUS ▼		DMC	ANCHOR	MADEIRA
.I.	Pale pink	3609	85	0710
·	Pale mauve	211	342	0801
⊣	Mauve	210	108	0802
–:	Medium mauve	554	97	0711
L	Purplish red*	315	896	0810
⊏	Pale blue	828	158	1101
	Blue*	340	118	0902
∴	Light green	3347	266	1408
+	Green	3346	262	1407
⊤	Dark green	3345	268	1406

Note: use purplish red* to separate petals and bks stamens, and blue* for bks outlining flower centre, separating it from the petals.

Chart 6 Field Scabious

Poppy Picture and Frame

The bright red of fragile poppies growing among stems of bearded barley is used here to create a striking picture. To complete the effect, the same design has been used for an eye-catching surround for a favourite photograph.

POPPY PICTURE
AND FRAME

YOU WILL NEED

For the Poppy picture, measuring 27cm × 22cm (10¾in × 8¾in) when framed:

33cm × 27.5cm (13in × 11in) of cream Aida, with 18 threads to 2.5cm (1in)
Stranded embroidery cotton in the colours given in the panel
No26 tapestry needle
Strong thread, for lacing across the back when mounting
Cardboard for mounting
Frame of your choice

For the photograph frame, measuring 27cm × 22cm (10¾in × 8¾in), with an aperture measuring 14cm × 9cm (5½in × 3½in):

25.5cm × 20.5cm (10¼in × 8¼in) of white perforated paper, with 14 holes to 2.5cm (1in)
Stranded embroidery cotton in the colours given in the panel
No24 tapestry needle
25.5cm × 20.5cm (10¼in × 8¼in) of iron-on interfacing
Frame of your choice

•

THE EMBROIDERY

For the picture, prepare the fabric and mark the horizontal and vertical centre lines with basting stitches in a light-coloured thread. Stretch the fabric in an embroidery frame, following the instructions on page 5. Begin at the centre and work out, using two strands of embroidery cotton in the needle for both cross stitch and backstitching. Gently steam press the finished embroidery.

For the frame, find the centre of the perforated paper by counting the spaces between holes. Mark this point with a soft pencil, and then count out to a convenient starting point on the border. Use three strands of embroidery cotton in the needle for both cross stitch and backstitching. When you have completed your design, cut out the central aperture. Mark the line first with a soft pencil and cut with a sharp craft knife.

MOUNTING AND FRAMING

For the picture, mark the central horizontal and vertical lines on the cardboard to be used for mounting and align these with the lines of basting stitches. Lace the embroidery over the mount, following the instructions on page 6, and remove basting stitches. Set the mount in a frame of your choice.

For the frame, iron the interfacing to the back of the embroidered perforated paper and then use a craft knife to trim the interfacing to the same size, including the aperture. Insert the embroidered paper into the frame of your choice.

POPPY PICTURE

POPPY FRAME

*Note: one skein of each colour will complete both designs, but if
you are only making the frame you will not require the dark
brown; poppy picture bks the stamens of the seed heads in black,
barley whiskers and soil in fawn, highlights on the seed pod in
yellowish green, lines separating the barley grains in cream, soil
in dark brown, and poppy bud stems in green; for the frame bks
barley whiskers in fawn, lines separating barley grains in cream,
tip of barley leaf in pale green, and poppy bud stems in green.*

	POPPIES	DMC	ANCHOR	MADEIRA
	Cream*	746	275	0101
⊣	Red	349	13	0212
⊐	Deep red	498	19	0511
⊿	Maroon	902	897	0601
∴	Light orange	608	330	0206
⌐	Orange red	606	335	0209
+	Deep orange	900	333	0208
T	Deep salmon	3340	329	0301
·	Pale green	3053	859	1510
⊱	Green	3347	266	1408
⊥	Medium green	3346	262	1407
⊤	Dark green	3345	268	1406
—	Yellowish green	472	264	1414
I	Fawn	372	887	2110
⊔	Dark brown	3031	905	2003
■	Black	310	403	Black

Sachets and Herb Pillow

What could be more delightful than a sweet-scented sachet to place in a drawer or wardrobe, or a fragrant herb pillow to help induce sleep? These sachets are easy to make and a pleasure to receive (if you can bear to part with them).

SACHETS AND
HERB PILLOW

YOU WILL NEED

For the Dog Violet pot pourri sack, measuring
9.5cm × 15.5cm (3¾in × 6¼in) approximately:

Two 14.5cm × 21cm (5¾in × 8½in) pieces of
beige Hardanger fabric, Rustico, with 18 threads
to 2.5cm (1in)
46cm (18in) of lilac ribbon, 12mm (½in) wide
Stranded embroidery cotton in the colours given
in the appropriate panel
No26 tapestry needle
Pot pourri of your choice for filling

For the Cornflower sachet, measuring 13cm (5in)
square, excluding the lace edging:

18cm (7¼in) square of cream Aida fabric, with 18
threads to 2.5cm (1in)
15cm (6in) square of cotton net, for backing
90cm (1yd) of cream lace edging, 18mm
(¾in) wide
46cm (18in) of lavender ribbon, for bow and loop
Stranded embroidery cotton in the colours given
in the appropriate panel
No26 tapestry needle
Pot pourri of your choice for filling

For the Ragged Robin herb pillow, measuring
21.5cm × 14cm (8½in × 5½in):

Two 27cm × 19.5cm (10¾in × 7¾in) pieces of
cream Aida fabric, with 18 threads to 2.5cm (1in)
70cm (27in) of cream lace edging, 18mm
(¾in) wide
Stranded embroidery cotton in the colours given
in the appropriate panel
No26 tapestry needle
Pot pourri of your choice for filling

THE EMBROIDERY

Prepare fabric, marking the centre lines of each
design with basting stitches, with the exception of
the pot pourri sack. For this, measure up 6cm
(2½in) from one short edge and baste a line across
from one side to the other. This marks the base line.

Mount the fabric in a hoop or frame, following
the instructions on page 5. Referring to the appropriate chart, complete the cross stitching, using two
strands of embroidery cotton in the needle for both
the cross stitch and the backstitching. For the pot
pourri sack, start from the centre of the base line.
For the other designs, start from the centre and
work out. Embroider the main areas first, and then
finish with the backstitching. Steam press on the
wrong side.

MAKING THE POT POURRI SACK

Place the two pieces of fabric with right sides
together and trim to measure 11.5cm × 18cm (4½in
× 7¼in). Taking a 12mm (½in) seam allowance,
stitch the side and bottom seams. Roll a narrow hem
around the top of the sack, stitching it by hand.

Fold the ribbon in half and, leaving a loop 5cm
(2in) long at the folded end, stitch it to the side of the
sack, about 3cm (1¼in) down from the top edge. Fill
the sack with pot pourri and tie the ribbon securely.

MAKING THE LACE-TRIMMED SACHET

Trim the embroidered fabric to measure 15cm (6in)
square. With right sides together, and taking a
12mm (½in) seam allowance, stitch it to the net,
leaving an opening of 6.5cm (2½in). Trim across the
corners; turn the sachet right side out and press the
edges.

Join the short edges of the lace with a small french
seam. Gather the lace and stitch it by hand to the
edge of the sachet, allowing extra fullness at the
corners. Decorate with a bow and loop of ribbon at
one corner.

Fill the sachet with pot pourri, and slipstitch the
opening.

MAKING THE HERB PILLOW

Trim the two pieces of fabric to measure 24.5cm ×
16.5cm (9½in × 6½in). With right sides together,
and taking a 12mm (½in) seam allowance, join the
two pieces, leaving a gap of 8cm (3½in) in one side.
Trim across the corners; turn the pillow right side
out, and press the edges. Add the lace, as for the
sachet; then fill with pot pourri or lavender, and
slipstitch the opening.

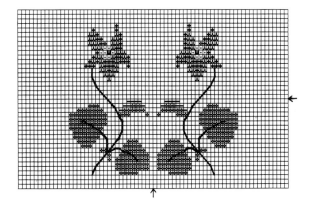

DOG VIOLET ▶	DMC	ANCHOR	MADEIRA
· Ecru	Ecru	926	Ecru
⌐ Pale mauve	554	97	0711
+ Mauve	208	110	0804
⊔ Reddish orange	350	11	0213
— Pale green	3364	260	1603
⋄ Dark green	3345	268	1406

Note: bks main stems in dark green and leaf rib in pale green.

CORNFLOWER ◀	DMC	ANCHOR	MADEIRA
· Pale mauve	210	108	0802
⊔ Light navy	336	150	1007
I Pale blue	341	117	0901
⋄ Blue	340	118	0902
⊤ Dark blue	793	121	0906
⊾ Green	3347	266	1408
+ Dark green	3345	268	1406

Note: bks in green.

RAGGED ROBIN ▼	DMC	ANCHOR	MADEIRA
· Ecru	Ecru	926	Ecru
⌐ Pale pink	3609	85	0710
⊥ Medium pink	3608	86	0709
✗ Deep pink	3607	87	0708
— Pale green	3348	264	1409
Green*	3347	266	1408
+ Dark green	3345	268	1406
⊔ Purplish brown	315	896	0810

Note: bks centres of two lower flowers in ecru, and bud stalks in purplish brown, all main stems in green, and centres of five upper flowers in pale green.*

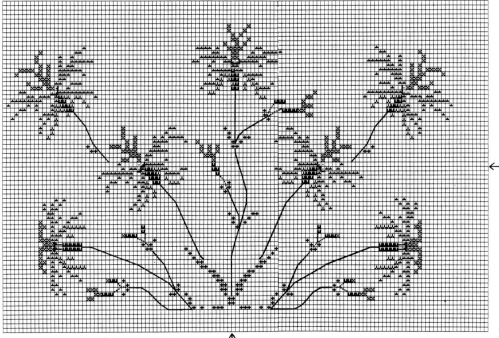

Pins and Needles

The vivid blue cornflower (*Centaurea cyanus*) provides a bold design for a pincushion. The diminutive and paler blue flowers of the forget-me-not (*Myosotis arvensis*) are used for the needlecase. These flowers have a yellow centre and are often a delicate pink in bud.

PINS AND NEEDLES

YOU WILL NEED

For the Forget-me-not needlecase, measuring
12.5cm × 11.5cm (5in × 4½in):

*33cm × 16.5cm (13in × 6½in) of cream Aida
fabric, with 18 threads to 2.5cm (1in)
27.5cm × 14cm (11in × 5½in) of satin lining fabric
25cm × 11.5cm (10in × 4½in) of heavyweight
iron-on interfacing
23cm × 9cm (9in × 3½in) of cream felt
45cm (18in) of matching ribbon, 6mm (¼in) wide
Stranded embroidery cotton in the colours given
in the appropriate panel
No26 tapestry needle*

For the Cornflower pincushion, measuring
10cm (4in) in diameter:

*23cm (9in) square of cream Aida fabric, with
18 threads to 2.5cm (1in)
Stranded embroidery cotton in the colours given
in the appropriate panel
No26 tapestry needle
Pincushion base and pad (for suppliers, see
page 48)*

•

THE EMBROIDERY

For the needlecase, first fold the fabric in two, to
measure 16.5cm (6½) square. With the fold on the
left, measure in 2.5cm (1in) from each raw edge
and mark the upper surface of the fabric at the top,
bottom and right-hand side with basting stitches.
The centre of the area enclosed by the fold and
basting lines is the centre point of the design.

For each design, prepare the fabric and set it in a
hoop (see pages 4-5). Embroider the design, using
two strands of thread in the needle for both the

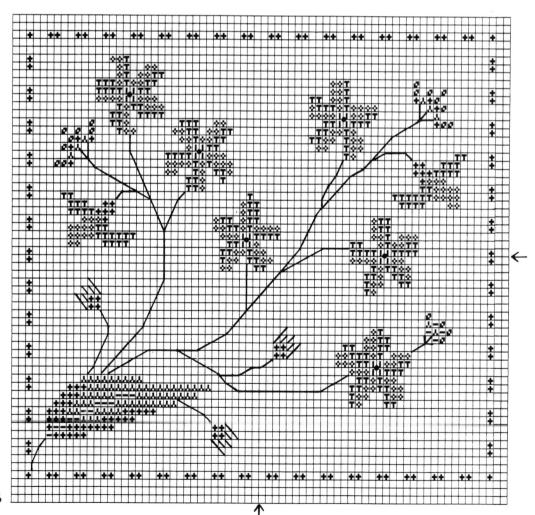

cross stitch and the backstitching. Gently press the finished embroidery on the wrong side.

FINISHING

For the needlecase, trim the fabric to measure 27.5cm × 14cm (11in × 5½in). Make and press a 12mm (½in) turning on all sides, mitring the corners. Slide the interfacing under the turnings and iron it in place.

Turn under 12mm (½in) all around the lining and hem it to cover the interfacing. Attach the felt to the inside of the case by lightly stitching down the centre. Tie the ribbon into a bow and use it to trim the spine.

For the pincushion, use a plate or similar round guide to trim the fabric to a 19cm (7½in) circle. Stitching 12mm (½in) from the edge, run a line of gathering stitches around the fabric. Place it over the pincushion dome and tighten until it fits snugly. Secure the thread firmly. Place the dome in the wooden base and screw firmly into position.

FORGET-ME-NOT ◄		DMC	ANCHOR	MADEIRA
I	Yellow	307	289	0104
⬩	Pale blue	794	120	0907
⊤	Blue	799	145	0910
♪	Purplish blue	340	118	0902
−	Pale green	3348	264	1409
⌐	Green	3347	266	1408
+	Dark green	3346	817	1407
	Light brown*	680	901	2210

Note: bks flower centres in light brown*, stems in dark green and buds in purplish blue.

CORNFLOWER ▼		DMC	ANCHOR	MADEIRA
·	Pale mauve	210	108	0802
⊔	Light navy	336	150	1007
I	Pale blue	341	117	0901
⬩	Blue	340	118	0902
⊤	Dark blue	793	121	0906
♪	Green	3347	266	1408
+	Dark green	3345	268	1406

ACKNOWLEDGEMENTS

I should like to thank my mother, Violet Watts, who made up or assembled all the embroidered articles illustrated in this book, and who patiently recorded the various steps she took and processes she employed for inclusion in the instructions for finishing the projects.

I should also like to thank Betty Haste who researched each of the flowers I have used in my designs, and who searched daily the local gardens, hedgerows and wasteland to find fresh and perfect specimens for me to work from.

Finally I must express my appreciation to friends and neighbours who followed the creation of these designs with such interest and gave me so much encouragement.

SUPPLIERS

The following mail order company has supplied some of the basic items needed for making up the projects in this book:

Framecraft Miniatures Limited
148-150 High Street
Aston
Birmingham, B6 4US
England
Telephone (021) 359 4442

Addresses for Framecraft stockists worldwide
Ireland Needlecraft Pty. Ltd.
2-4 Keppel Drive
Hallam, Victoria 3803
Australia

Danish Art Needlework
PO Box 442, Lethbridge
Alberta T1J 3Z1
Canada

Sanyei Imports
PO Box 5, Hashima Shi
Gifu 501-62
Japan

The Embroidery Shop
286 Queen Street
Masterton
New Zealand

Anne Brinkley Designs Inc.
246 Walnut Street
Newton
Mass. 02160
USA

S A Threads and Cottons Ltd.
43 Somerset Road
Cape Town
South Africa

For information on your nearest stockist of embroidery cotton, contact the following:

DMC

UK
DMC Creative World Limited
62 Pullman Road
Wigston
Leicester, LE8 2DY
Telephone: 0533 811040

USA
The DMC Corporation
Port Kearney Bld.
10 South Kearney
N.J. 07032-0650
Telephone: 201 589 0606

AUSTRALIA
DMC Needlecraft Pty
P.O. Box 317
Earlswood 2206
NSW 2204
Telephone: 02599 3088

COATS AND ANCHOR

UK
Kilncraigs Mill
Alloa
Clackmannanshire
Scotland, FK10 1EG
Telephone: 0259 723431

USA
Coats & Clark
P.O. Box 27067
Dept CO1
Greenville
SC 29616
Telephone: 803 234 0103

AUSTRALIA
Coats Patons Crafts
Thistle Street
Launceston
Tasmania 7250
Telephone: 00344 4222

MADEIRA

UK
Madeira Threads (UK) Limited
Thirsk Industrial Park
York Road, Thirsk
N. Yorkshire, YO7 3BX
Telephone: 0845 524880

U.S.A.
Madeira Marketing Limited
600 East 9th Street
Michigan City
IN 46360
Telephone: 219 873 1000

AUSTRALIA
Penguin Threads Pty Limited
25-27 Izett Street
Prahran
Victoria 3181
Telephone: 03529 4400